DELERE

THIS   PAPERBACK   EDITION   FIRST
PUBLISHED IN 2015 BY DELERE PRESS LLP

ISG   ©   JEREMY   FERNANDO
IHOLE   ©   JULIAN   GOUGH
INTRODUCTION   ©   NEIL   MURPHY
PHOTOGRAPHS   ©   TAN   JINGLIANG
*   *   *
FIRST   PUBLISHED   IN   2015   BY
DELERE   PRESS   LLP

WWW.DELEREPRESS.COM
DELERE PRESS LLP REG NO. T11LL1061K

ISBN   978-981-09-4767-5

AN APPLE
A DAY ...

by Jeremy
Fernando & Julian
Gough, with
photographs by
Tan Jingliang, and
an introduction by
Neil Murphy

For Maya, Nadia, Lia, Dylan, and Sophie —

the beautiful ones.

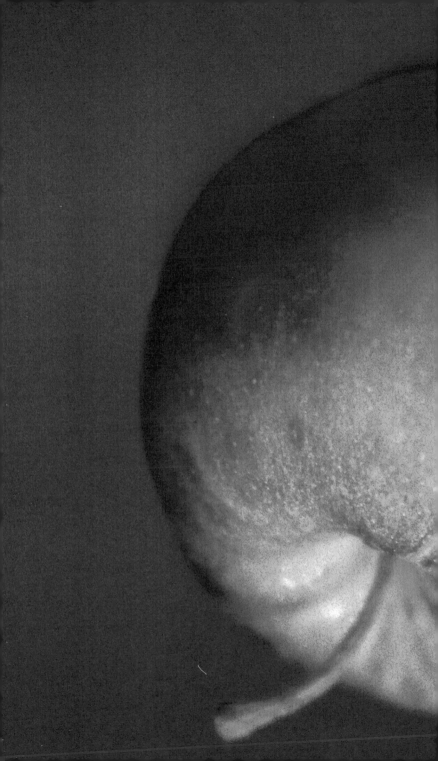

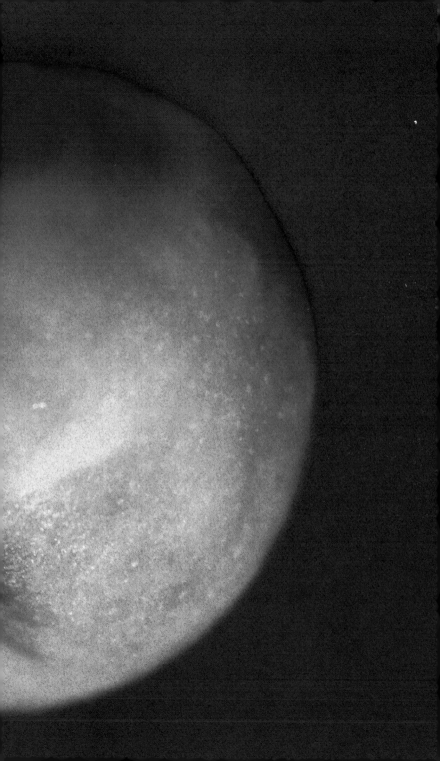

Introduction: When Thought Wanders Off

by

Neil Murphy

"There's no iHole like your own iHole"[1]

Neither Jeremy Fernando nor Julian Gough are *literally* concerned with the nominal subjects of their respective contributions to this book; that much seems clear, if anything can be clear in the face of their extravagant attempts to take perhaps the dominant icon of contemporary capitalism — the iPhone (and its variants) — and allow it to mutate into a prickly, resonant metaphor for everything from September 11, ISIS, Anders Behring Breivik, blind gratification, the power of the image, and being itself.

If Fernando is correct when he insists that his subjects are merely "manifestations of the same thing," and

1 Neil Murphy. 'Introduction: When Thought Wanders Off' in Fernando & Gough. *an apple a day...*, Delere Press, 2015: 9-14. This is a quasi-Anglicized variation of the Gaelic "Níl aon tóin tinn mar do thóin tinn féin," a correct translation of which can be found by using one's iPhone.

his iconic, compelling images of our time seem to sing the same tune, then we must look beyond them to find their commanding spirit. Gough provides a kind of answer in the instant gratification, the mad desire and love for the iHole even though people don't actually have "a task that requires it," coupled with the extraordinary beauty of the compelling (invisible) image that it generates. Gough's iHole is successfully launched, we are told, because it is done so "beautifully," even though it is unnecessary — what can be more unnecessary than a hole that eats away at the metaphorical substance of the world? And the essential, captivating madness of the unnamable space *beyond* the iHole's greedy membrane haunts both of the pieces in this book, despite their apparent differences.

Gough's "The iHole" is itself a tapestry, a remaking of a spirit that its author undoubtedly discovers elsewhere, especially in the scientific fascination and mesmerising, unorthodox spatiality of Flann O'Brien's *The Third Policeman*. O'Brien's spatially impossible police station, and otherworldly "Eternity," induce a similar sense of dislocation to the barely imaginable (but emphatically real) dimensions of the portable black hole that allows people to dump their trash, dead bodies, German tourists, Palestinians, and mothers into a universe beyond human jurisdiction, and ontological comprehension. Similarly, the matter-of-fact challenge to encyclopedic reality that Gough's story represents is also reminiscent of fictions like Barthelme's postmodern masterpiece, "The Balloon", itself a tale that toys with the human compulsion to impose meaning on the world, on impossible occurrences, and the fictional possibilities that are realised when the two converge. An iHole, after all, with all of its lunacy-generating desire, is metaphorically just a hair's breadth away from an iPhone with *its* encoded encyclopedia of imprinted desires. Gough's story is not simply irreverent to capitalism's toys, it also seeks to pulverise flat notions of material reality by provoking and disturbing them and, in so doing, fulfills one of the central possibilities of the creative impulse. As Raymond Federman claims, of the branch of innovative fiction to which Gough's surely belongs, it "constantly renews our faith in man's imagination and not in man's distorted vision of reality," and "reveals man's irrationality rather than man's rationality."[2]

And this is precisely the point where Fernando's diagnosis of contemporary 'reality', if that isn't too explicit a term for what he seeks to name, meets Gough's. Federman's appreciation of a kind of fiction that permits the irrational to speak, that allows the imaginative impulse to subvert the purely rational, can be extended beyond the fictive realm (wherever that actually ends). This is Fernando's territory: he questions societies' self-preserving habitual responses to acts

2 Raymond Federman 'Prefatory Note' in *Surfiction: Fiction Now and Tomorrow.* edited by Raymond Federman. Chicago: Swallow, 1975: 7-8.

of apparent irrationality, which are commanded by the rules of reason. As a result, the irrational is re-packaged, often, ironically, in indefinable terms like evil or insanity; the *other* is thus named and domesticated. Fernando's larger target, of course, is meaning, or our attempts to force the meaningless into the garb of meaning — although this doesn't simply extend to a different kind of avoidance. He just wants to keep the monster in the game, lest we forget we are monsters.

And they are necessary monsters.

For Fernando, via Fynsk, this amounts to retaining "a position of openness to the fullness of possibility — and nothing else," while to Gough, via by-now-established iHole law, "[i]f an event occurs within the boundary [of the world on the other side of the iHole's membrane], information from that event cannot reach an outside observer, making it impossible to determine if such an event occurred." Perhaps, after all, that is why we need artistic fictions (and Fernando is a fiction-maker every bit as much as Gough) because, at their best, they allow thought to wander off, "in sweet lazy liberty," as Kundera has it;[3] they permit us to live with monsters in realms where merely sequential, linear, thought can't go. Borges too knew this. Citing Schopenhauer, and writing of the value of placing worlds within worlds, zones within

---

3 Milan Kundera. 'Jerusalem Address: Europe and the Novel' in *The Art of the Novel, London, Faber & Faber, 1988*: 162.

zones in artistic forms, he reminds us of the fullness, the essential oneness, of allowing *mythos* and *logos* to live together in our minds: "Arthur Schopenhauer wrote that dreaming and wakefulness are the pages of a single book, and that to read them in order is to live, and to leaf through them at random, to dream. Paintings within paintings and books that branch into other books help us to sense this oneness."[4] Both Gough and Fernando offer elegant acts of resistance to the merely ordered, and in so doing they invite us to dream beyond the permissible.

Neil Murphy
January 2015
Singapore

---

4 Jorge Luis Borges. 'When Fiction Lives in Fiction' in *Selected Non-Fictions*. edited by Eliot Weinberger. New York: Penguin, 1999: 162.

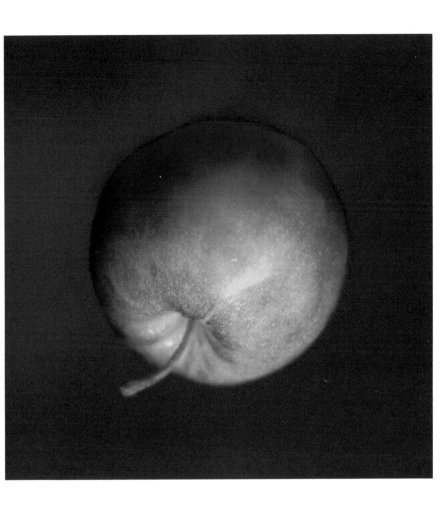

The iHole.
by Julian
Gough

This is the original version of the 'iHole', never previously printed. This version was shortlisted for the BBC International Short Story Award, but the BBC lawyers were very nervous about mentioning Apple, Steve, Johnny Ive, etc. — and so it was changed before broadcast.

Here is the uncut version.

Original Apple flavour.

It was a presentation Tuesday, and the room was full. While they waited for Thierry, they ran through a year's worth of rumours. He'd moved back in with his mother. His mother was schizophrenic. No, she'd lost her memory in a carcrash. She collected, ah, butterflies? Barbies? Beanie Babies. She'd been seen wandering around a parking lot, naked... But the rumours had low energy, and soon died out. Thierry himself had no enemies, no friends, and no life that anyone knew of.

****

He'd unveiled it before most people had noticed he was in the room.

The black hole sat there, floating in mid air, beside the lectern.

Eventually somebody said "…But what does it do?"

Thierry scratched the back of his neck. "Uh, it kind of doesn't matter what it does. Everyone will want one. Look at it."

They looked at it. It was beautiful.

Sharif, from the hardware engineering team, reached towards it. Stopped. "What about the interface?" he said. "You can't really touch it, can you?"

"No. But I've already talked to Jonathan, and he doesn't think that'll be a problem."

"Why can I see it?" said Melissa from the strategy group.

"Positive and negative uh particles…" Of course, Melissa's background was in physics. Thierry restarted. "Matter and antimatter particle pairs come into existence all the time, everywhere, you know—vacuum energy—but usually they annihilate each other straight away."

"Like the Oilers and the Flames," said Brett, ever the professional Canadian. Nobody laughed, they didn't even acknowledge it, they wanted to hear Thierry.

"Um, this is designed to suck in the antimatter, and push away the, the matter. So it radiates. But the radiation is coming from just *outside* the Schwarzschild radius, the event horizon, you see? Nothing can come back from inside the, uh, Schwarzschild radius."

"But..." Melissa was frowning. "Hawking discovered that small black holes evaporate, no?"

"Only incredibly small ones. And besides, if it's losing mass you can just feed it."

Melissa nodded. "Have you… fed it?"

"Uh, not yet."

Melissa leaned towards it. "Can I?"

"Sure."

Melissa picked up Thierry's pen from the lip of the lectern. Thierry's body almost made to reach for the pen, but only twitched slightly, as his mind cancelled the order. It was just a pen.

"So, anyway," said Thierry. "It's spinning, so it's stable, like a gyroscope…."

Melissa threw Thierry's pen through the air. It vanished into the black hole.

"Oh my God," said Melissa. "That felt..." She shook her head. "These are going to be huge… Do it," Melissa urged the others. "Do it…"

It was a very clean space. No trash cans, no trash. People began to look through their pockets for old tissues, ringpulls, candy wrappers. They dropped them, threw them, flicked them into the black hole. Each time, a gasp, or startled laughter.

"Why doesn't it fall?" said Sharif. "I mean it has a lot of mass, right?"

"That was the hardest part. It's designed to radiate boundary energy asymmetrically—

downwards—enough to balance gravity. It's constantly making very fine adjustments, like a Segway."

"Is it safe?"

"There are safety features. Filters. You don't want kids falling into them. It's too small to swallow anything larger or heavier than, you know, a melon. Anything bigger will just bounce back."

"What about your finger?"

"If it's attached to you, it'll bounce back. It registers the whole mass."

"So you'd have to cut up your victims," said Brett.

Thierry smiled uneasily.

They drifted away, excited, a little giddy. Thierry was right; they all wanted one.

****

Steve got his own private presentation the next day, and he made it a priority project. They assembled a team around Thierry. A lot of technicians under him, and some senior managers unobtrusively over him. Let's say, alongside him.

Over the next few weeks, they perfected it. Jonathan came in with his team, and they radically improved the interface. Made it more sensitive to human-scale movement. Now you could move it around with hand gestures. It could follow you like a balloon.

****

The prototypes were kept under the usual high security in the new building. But the original, by unspoken agreement, Thierry was allowed keep. It floated over the white leather top of his new desk. He didn't put anything into it himself. But people would wander by, from every corner of the campus. They'd chat for a minute, then say they didn't want to disturb him, but could they… He'd nod, and they'd throw something into it. A soda can, a cigarette butt. Sometimes something wrapped up, or hidden with a hand. And then the big sigh of relief, or the sudden laugh, at the oddness, the finality, of putting anything into the black hole. The *satisfaction*.

"Well, it's not like any normal means of disposal," Thierry would say politely.

"Yes!" They'd be giddy. "It feels like I blasted it beyond the solar system," "…beyond the edge of the galaxy," "…beyond the rim of the known universe."

"Yes," he'd say. " You did. It is removed from the universe."

****

Technically, things went pretty smoothly. The biggest arguments were about what to call it. What seemed the only obvious name to Thierry was fiercely contested by some of the marketing department. In the end, Steve over-ruled marketing. "People will hate the name. Sure. So what? It's simple and it works. People hated the name iPad, for about a week. They made every possible joke about sanitary towels—for a week. And then they got used to it."

****

Steve launched it in February. He did it beautifully.

****

Thierry celebrated that night. The team took him to a bar in the hills west of Cupertino. Around 2am, he was standing outside, looking up at the stars. The black hole floated over his head. He tried to line it up with Sirius. There. The black hole bent the starlight around itself, making a tiny ring of light.

He felt his vision flashing, and he looked down, bewildered, at the joint in his right hand. Who'd given it to him? He brought it up to his eyes. Was it laced with something? The white paper, the smoke, seemed to turn blue, then red, then blue. By the time he realised it was a cop car's lights, it was too late, they had the camera on him and were filming. He flicked the joint, reflexively, toward the black hole, and it vanished from the universe.

The cops took him in and tried to frighten him for the next two, three hours, but he was very relaxed and waited it out. He had nothing on him. They let him go at dawn. He picked up the original iHole at the front desk. The young cop on duty, who'd been playing with it, feeding it paperclips, said, "So when can I get one of these?" and Thierry gave him the tour.

****

The previews, working off the specifications Steve had announced at the launch, were sniffy as hell. Why would anyone want this? The price is all wrong. It doesn't do anything a garbage can doesn't do better, for less.

But the reviews, once people had actually tried one, were raves.

Apple shipped a million iHoles, and they were sold out pretty much everywhere in three days. And the word of mouth was incredible.

****

A month later, Pogue, in the New York Times, wrote a sober and considered piece that basically said, it isn't perfect, but they will iterate it. Look at all the things missing from the first iPod, iPhone, iPad. "But already it has replaced the office shredder, wastepaper baskets, your garbage can, ashtrays... Not just replaced. It's made the act of disposal sexy. My kids fight to take out the trash, and they dispose of it eggshell by eggshell, they don't want it to be over. When people love a device so much that they want to play with it, even when they don't actually have a task that requires it… the device works. The iHole is going to be a huge, global hit."

And it was.

****

People started to bring out attachments, add-ons. You could connect your iHole to the back of your mower. Watch the grass fly up, curve around it, and… vanish. One attachment—with a little ramp, a cheeseholder—turned it into a better mousetrap.

****

When the iHole 2 came out, they'd made its sensors much, much more fine-grained. Now it could tell the difference between you and the crumbs on your hands, the sand in your cracks, dandruff in your hair. You could set the filters to clean yourself with it. You could be so clean it was as though you'd never really been clean before.

****

The only negative reactions came from the environmental movement, but even they found it hard to find an angle, a tone. They came off as attacking it just because it was new.

There was something close to a backlash, when the recycling companies started to go out of business. But Apple immediately ran ads showing how much landfill would be unnecessary if everybody carried an iHole. The number of incinerators that wouldn't need to be built. Smiling children played in green fields as their father dropped the picnic rubbish into the family iHole. Then Apple tweaked the iHole 4 so that it absorbed carbon dioxide from the air around it. And dropped the price of the entry model by a hundred dollars. At the launch, Steve painted it as the ultimate carbon capture device. Green resistance collapsed. Apple's share price doubled.

****

Then the scare stories started running. It had taken a while—iHoles were as close to tamper-proof as consumer products could get—but now people were modifying them. A man in Brazil—upset after his girlfriend left him for a woman—managed to stick his penis in a jail-broken iHole, with highly unpleasant consequences. Which he filmed for her. The clip was the most viewed in the world that year.

****

The first big court case involved a woman in New Jersey who'd modified an array of iHoles to take massive objects. She ran the operation out of a warehouse, and got caught when the stream of dumptrucks started blocking the docks. She was charged with running an unlicensed landfill. Apple were subpoenaed, as accessories.

There were months of tortuous argument, from dozens of expert witnesses. It went all the way to the Supreme Court, with more and more parties joining the case.

Liberal groups, worried about the abortion implications, defended the right to dispose of whatever you like on private property. They also argued that garbage disposal was a form of speech, protected by the First Amendment. Conservatives defended private ownership of modified iHole arrays on Second Amendment grounds.

Thierry followed the case with decreasing interest. Halfway through the Supreme Court hearing, the judges had requested iHoles, in order to understand the case. It was quite obvious they'd fallen in love with theirs instantly, and were clearly not going to rule against Apple.

After a lot of closing evidence from physicists, the case was dismissed on the grounds that, even if there had been a crime, it had not been committed in this universe.

****

The first knockoffs were announced at the Consumer Electronics Show, in Las Vegas, a few weeks later. But there were stability issues, and none of the products which were announced that January made it to market that summer.

Microsoft had learned a lesson from the failure of their answer to the iPod. The Zune had sold poorly through online shops, partly because it was always last in any alphabetical list of similar products. Senior executives at Microsoft were anxious not to make that mistake again. They over-ruled their marketing department, and in late September launched the A-Hole.

But it was already too late. The iHole completely owned the market. Even expensive, well thought-out competitors were perceived as cheap, inferior copies. In the run-up to Christmas, desperate for market share, Microsoft began to sell their A-Hole at a loss. They still couldn't get penetration.

****

The unauthorised modifications began to get out of hand. In a global marketplace, this threw up some cultural differences. That autumn, in Canada, people used it to get rid of leaves.

In the USA and Mexico, the number of people found murdered dropped sharply. The number reported missing rose.

In China, protests in rural areas ceased to be a problem.

In Saudi Arabia, Wahabi extremists dropped Shias, German tourists, and the wrong kinds of Sunni down the hole—slowly, headfirst—and posted the videos online.

In the West Bank, settlers threw Palestinians down the hole (except on Saturdays). And vice versa (except on Fridays).

In Gaza, Hamas and Fatah spent most of their budgets on iHoles, and threw each other down the hole in such quantities that Gaza became quite peaceful, until an Israeli soldier threw a Palestinian teenager down the hole at a border crossing, and it all kicked off again.

A number of lawsuits emerged from all this. But Apple made no admission of liability, and were cleared in every case. The US Supreme Court's precedent proved extremely useful. In country after country, the entire product was deemed to exist, by definition, beyond the event horizon, and therefore beyond the jurisdiction of the court, whose jurisdiction was limited to this universe.

****

At the end of the year, the amount of money Thierry received in his bonus was ridiculous. He celebrated by going to the bank, withdrawing a million dollars in cash, and throwing it, a hundred dollars at a time, into the original iHole. Then he smashed up all his furniture and fed in the pieces.

On his way to the bar that night, the cops stopped him. He thought it was to do with his mother, but it was for pot again. He was so relieved, he let them find some.

Afterwards, when the court summons arrived, he regretted it. Too late.

To avoid thinking about the court case, he lost himself in research, helping Jonathan Ive work on the big problem. Eventually they solved it, by shifting the Hawking radiation into the visible spectrum. Cautiously, tweak by tweak, they turned a black hole white.

The next iteration had hardly any functional improvements, but it came out in white, and the world upgraded. Within a month, kids with the original black iHole were being jeered at in the street. Their hats, their lunch, their homework were shoved down the hole.

****

Back in court, Thierry felt proceedings weren't really real. He'd opted for jury trial. The judge and the lawyers on both sides seemed to be playing language games. Thierry couldn't see how their arguments related to empirical, objective reality. They just seemed to be sentences about paragraphs of old laws that had been written with no understanding of the strangeness and beauty of the universe.

He modified his iHole as the jury deliberated. When they came back into court and announced that they had reached their verdict, he gently lobbed his modified iHole into the jury box, and they all disappeared.

This led to a second, more serious courtcase. But precedent in iHole law was by now clear: "If an event occurs within the boundary, information from that event cannot reach an outside observer, making it impossible to determine if such an event occurred."

The judge in Thierry's second case determined that the first jury had reached a verdict but that it was not known yet, therefore could not be acted upon. As a verdict had been reached in the original trial, there could be no second trial. However, Thierry was ordered to restore the settings on his iHole to their original state. He did so.

Thierry was released.

****

Back at home, he didn't seem to know what to do. The house was just a shell with a futon lying on the floor of one room. Using his Swiss army knife, Thierry ripped up the futon and fed it into the black hole. It took all night.

****

At dawn, he brought the iHole to the lab and let himself in. The cleaners stared at him. He said hello, quietly. He sat at his desk, in his imposing chair, and looked at the iHole for a while. He'd stuck with the original black so long, it was coming back into fashion as a retro look.

He slowly logged into the iHole's core code, through layer after layer of security.

He modified the source code for all iHoles worldwide, and sent it out as an emergency security patch/update.

Something fell back out of the iHole, and bounced across the desk.

He picked it up, and looked at it. His pen. He brought the tip down to the desk's surface, and scribbled. After a hesitant, scratchy second or so, the ink came through. He stared at the tight black scribble on the white leather.

A Snickers wrapper fell on the leather beside him. Then another. As the candy wrappers and used tissues and Coke cans fell all around him, bouncing off his back, his arms, his bowed head, he wrote "I'm sorry I'm sorry I'm sorry I'm sorry I'm sorry," on the white leather desk, till the pen ran out of ink and the dry tip tore holes in the white skin.

Eventually the first Beanie Baby fell onto the desk. He threw the empty pen into the corner of the room, curled up in the big chair, and waited for his mother to return.

iS6
by Jeremy
Fernando

*iPhone 6 and iPhone 6 Plus are the
biggest advancements in iPhone
history … And once again Apple is
poised to captivate the world with a
revolutionary product …*

— Tim Cook[1]

*[The United States will join] with our
friends and allies to degrade, and
ultimately destroy, the terrorist group
known as ISIL.*

— Barack Obama[2]

Declarations which bear echoes of a similar one on the 2nd of May, 2011; one that had generated a similar amount of excitement: the murder of Osama bin Laden.

And here, we should not forget that what had captivated us was not so much bin Laden's death — after all, one could argue that his killing had been coming for years, that it was a matter of time — but his abode. For, contrary to popular belief, he was not holed-up in a cave but living rather comfortably in a resort-like fortress. And, if we had been shown an aerial view of his compound — without knowing that it were in the middle of Abbottabad, Pakistan — we would have probably assumed that it was a holiday villa of a rich — perhaps slightly paranoid — businessman.

Perhaps then, what had really shocked us was the fact that it revealed a little too clearly what September 11th was: *capitalism at its purest.*

A testament to decentralisation, coordination, maximum media impact.

With images of planes crashing into the Twin Towers on re-run testifying to the success of the event.

For, in that instant Al-Qaeda established brand monopoly over terrorism; becoming an overnight sensation, a household name, as it were.

The proof of their astounding success was repeatedly demonstrated in the ensuing decade, where any act of terror against states was promptly credited to Al-Qaeda; until someone else claimed responsibility, after which that said group would be linked to them. The proverbial icing on the cake though lies in the fact that whenever anyone utters 'September 11th', there is never a need to state the year — that particular day in 2001 seems to have swallowed every other year in history.

In the intervening decade, many had been concerned that the killing of bin Laden would be a strategic error: a common argument is he would be turned into a martyr — which is precisely what he always wanted. After which, bin Laden would become a symbol around which the entire terror network could revolve.

But this is where they completely missed the point.

We were way beyond that already.

For, even as the planes were crashing into the Twin Towers, Osama bin Laden had already become the master-signifier for terrorism; and from that point onwards, his spectre has been haunting the world. Thus, killing him makes — has since made — absolutely no difference. In fact, his enemies probably profited from the fact that he was found lounging in a villa-like resort: imagine the brand optimisation if bin Laden was actually found in a cave.

To compound matters, bin Laden's killing only demonstrated how much Al-Qaeda epitomises a multi-national corporation. His succession was almost instantaneous: on June 16, Al-Qaeda issued a press release officially declaring Ayman al-Zawahiri its new leader.[3] An echo of which was not too difficult to hear in August 2011, when Steve Jobs resigned as head of Apple Inc. In fact, a paragraph from *The Wall Street Journal* — "Mr. Jobs has developed a cult-like following among both employees and customers who hang on his every word at press conferences and vigorously defend the executive from those who might question his products" — could well have been a eulogy for bin Laden.[4] What remains crucial for us is: in terms of operations, the day after — May 3, 2011 — was like any other day; this being the true test of a corporation: the ability to continue without its founder.

An instance of the echo of the *eternal corpus* — the King is dead, long live the King — resounding in corporations: it matters not who is head; they are all manifestations of the same thing.

Thus, FOX News' error on May 2, 2011 — when they declared, "Obama bin Laden is dead" — turns out to be a perfect reading of the situation.

For, in this game, *everyone is perfectly exchangeable.*

Terrorism, like viruses, is everywhere.
There is a global perfusion of
terrorism, which accompanies any
system of domination as though it
were its shadow, ready to activate
itself anywhere like a double
agent. We can no longer draw a
demarcation line around it. It is at
the very heart of this culture which
combats it …

— Jean Baudrillard[5]

And it is "everywhere" not just because it can be anywhere, at any place, but more importantly, it can be whatever you want it to be.

ISIL — ISIS — IS
I can be anything you want me to be.
Put in me all your fears, your desires.
Perhaps even your dreams.

And terrorism — perhaps unbeknownst to the terrorists themselves — has taken a leaf out of HIV's playbook: the best way to overcome opposition is not to fight it head-on, directly, but to use its own defenses against itself.

Which might be why publicised beheadings, televised executions, seem to be the Islamic State's weapon of choice: for, it is nothing other than the turning of the notion of *free dissemination of information* — the very notion that the so-called Occidental world holds so dearly — against itself. And the reaction of the West is to, rather predictably, call for a stop to the circulation of these videos: in other words, self-censorship; a curtailing of the freedom of expression, of free media, which its very identity — or, more importantly, the illusion on which its identity — is built upon.

And this — as Slavoj Žižek will never let us forget — is the lesson of Stalinism: *even if everyone knows it is a performance, it is crucial to keep up, maintain, appearances.* Which is why, at show trials — even when every one knows that the trial is nothing but a show — it was mandatory for the condemned to confess to their crimes. For, this allowed everyone to maintain the illusion that there was a trial taking place; much like how censorship does nothing other than to protect the illusion of innocence. After all, it is not as if one cannot find what has been deleted somewhere else. Moreoever, the effects of the unseen but suggested — the implied — are often stronger than what is shown, displayed.

However, one must bear in mind that it is not so much that we can live with lies: it is more so that *it is lies we need in order to live*. For, it is not that we cannot tell that it is an illusion: it is that *illusions are crucial, not just to sustain a fantasy, but the very reality in which we live*.

And by censoring these images of public — media — executions, the so-called Western world is doing nothing other than preserving the illusion that one has the freedom of expression: precisely by declaring that certain expressions, images, are beyond the pale. Thus, it is not so much that you are not free to say, to show, these things, but that these things are the non-sayable, non-seeable; beyond the pale of what is to be said or unsaid, seen or unseen. So, it is not that one in the modern free Western world cannot express it, but that such images go against the very fibre of Western civilisation itself.

However, one must keep in mind that attempting to redefine what is permissable — what is admissable and what is *sans papiers* — is always already to rewrite, reconstitute, what it means to be civilised, to be *free*, itself. It is to admit more and more exclusions to protect the illusion of inclusiveness, increasing excisions to maintain the fantasy of openess.

The effects of this frantic, misguided, reaction could already be seen — admittedly, perhaps only retrospectively — in 2001; set in motion by none other than George W. Bush himself when he exclaimed, "these acts of mass murder were intended to frighten our nation into chaos and retreat. But they have failed. Our country is strong."[6] Never quite expecting that it is precisely the "steel of American resolve" to defend "the foundation of America" that turned — is continuing to turn— the US against itself.

For, what else is a return to 'roots', 'core values', but fundamentalism.

And there is quite possibly no phrase that encapsulates this situation more aptly than the title of Sarah Palin's memoir, *Going Rogue: An American Life*. For, this succinctly brings together the fact that both the alleged enemies of the US, the so called 'rogue elements', and the American way of life are basically the same. And here, it is not too difficult to hear Žižek's constant reminder that the pictures of torture scenes in Abu Gharaib prison resemble many initiation rites of college fraternities; in which "the Iraqi prisoners were effectively initiated into American culture."[7]

Perhaps, this is why the enduring image of September 11th is that of the smoldering Twin Towers: both Al-Qaeda and the US are mirror images of each other.

And perhaps both the *free world* and the so-called
fundamentalists — it could be IS, it could be Al
Qaeda, it could really be anyone — are not quite as
different as they, and we, would like to believe.

And if the opposite, the antonym, the Other, has
quite possibly disappeared, this suggests that not
only might one never quite be able to point out who
the enemy is, one might — we might — never quite
know if the enemy is within us, if the enemy is even
precisely us.

*Because you know the truth. You
know that somewhere down the road,
the truth always trumps everything.
And yesterday felt like the day it did.*

— Tim Cook[8]

And herein lies the crux to Tim Cook's promise to
"captivate the world," to revolutionise our lives.

By making everything Apple.

Where, "the next chapter for us is about personal
devices, about something that's even more personal
than what we had before. And I think the watch is a
great place to start that. And it has a lot of tentacles."
Where with "an object that is attached to you," you
not only have "the ability to control things … but you
might use your imagination on where that can be."[9]

Where imagination and control are no longer
opposing forces, but go hand in hand: described
— almost poetically — by Cook as "an intimacy in
connection and communication."

The truth has triumphed.

"The right doctrine has been implanted into these children."[10]

Our apostles will proselytise.

Not forgetting that there is always a way to pay for it.

"If you desire what God has promised, then set out in jihad for his cause."

— Abu Bakr al-Baghdadi[11]

*Terrorism is immoral … and it is a
response to a globalisation which is
itself immoral. So, let us be immoral;
and if we want to have some
understanding of all of this, let us go
and take a little look beyond Good
and Evil. When, for once, we have
an event that defies not just morality,
but any form of interpretation, let us
approach it with an understanding of
Evil (l'intelligence du Mal).*

— Jean Baudrillard[12]

For, the instant reaction, when confronted with any
situation — let alone an event — is to attempt to
explain the incident. Whether the reasons given are
true or not, are perhaps irrelevant: the fact of there
being a reason, a cause, is better than if there were
none. Which might be why conspiracy theories
are so popular: underlying them is the logic that
someone — no matter how implausible — is in
control. Which suggests that it is often easier to rely
on reason — no matter how fictive — than to not
have anything to cling onto. In many ways, it is even

better if the reason is fictional: for, if grounded in a certain fact, or reality, it can then go away. However, if it is in the realm of the imaginary, it is then always already metaphorical: thus, can be applied to any and every situation. And it is this, to echo Friedrich Nietzsche, that gives us us the *metaphysical comfort* that we can know what is going on.

> Even if it is a device,
> an operating system,
> a watch.

And here, it might be helpful to recall that *to watch* entails *sight* — even if only in the mind's eye. Quite possibility the seeing (*theoros*, spectator) that all theorising (*thea,* a view + *horan,* to see) entails. In which this "revolution" is an attempt to "captivate the world" by presenting, representing — bringing everything before one.

For, nothing scares us more than a lack of meaning — in particular, it is the inability to know in general that truly scares us. For, if we are unable to legitimately make a general statement, this suggests that we can never actually posit beyond a singular, situational, moment. Hence, we can never claim to know anything, anyone: at best, we can only catch momentary glimpses.

And, it is for this very reason that the initial psychiatric assessment — that Anders Behring Breivik is criminally insane — was the one that horrified us most. Not because we were concerned with whether he was actually responsible for his actions or not: the public was baying for his blood — had already held him accountable — anyway. But, more importantly, that if Breivik were insane, it would foreground our inability to understand, know. And as Aristotle has taught us, it is more important that something is plausible than if something were possible: in this context, we would rather have had Breivik as a calculating mass murderer than someone who was completely out of his mind.

This is especially ironic in light of the fact that none of us would claim to have any similarity with Breivik. Thus, the declaration that he was mad should be no more than a logical consequence. However, we also want Breivik to be legally accountable for his actions. And in order for that to be so, he needed to be of sound mind.

But if that were true, we can then no longer distinguish ourselves from him.

And it is precisely this that scares us.

For, we are horrified not when there are abnormalities to our way of life as there are two common reactions to this: either oppose and destroy

it or subsume it under the dominant logic. Which
can be seen most clearly, almost all too clearly,
in many responses to immigration; where there
are either calls for immigrants to 'pack up and
leave' or pseudo-liberal notions of 'we are all alike'.
Both of which are perverse versions of *all men are
brothers*: the brutal translation of which is that you
are my brother if you live in the same way as me;
otherwise, not only are you not my brother, you are
also potentially not part of mankind. This is played
out in our age of what is often termed *post-political
bio-politics*, a horribly awkward phrase that Žižek —
channeling Giorgio Agamben — unpacks rather
elegantly: "*post-politics* is a politics which claims to
leave behind old ideological struggles and, instead,
focus[es] on expert management and administration,
while *bio-politics* designates the regulation of the
security and welfare of human lives as its primary
goal."[13] He continues: "post-political bio-politics
also has two aspects which cannot but appear to
belong to two opposite ideological spaces: that of the
reduction of humans to 'bare life,' to *Homo sacer*, that
so-called sacred being who is the object of expert
caretaking knowledge, but is excluded, like prisoners
at Guantanamo or Holocaust victims, from all rights;
and that of respect for the vulnerable Other brought
to an extreme through an attitude of narcissistic
subjectivity which experiences the self as vulnerable,
constantly exposed to a multitude of potential
harassments [....] What these two poles share is
precisely the underlying refusal of any higher causes,

the notion that the ultimate goal of our lives is life itself. That is why there is no contradiction between the respect for the vulnerable Other and […] the extreme expression of treating individuals as *Homini sacer*."[14]

This might well be why the ones that are often harshest towards new immigrants are recently naturalised citizens. For, if there is no longer any "ideological struggle" and all life is reduced to mere automation — and people from living beings to automatons — there is the realisation that we are all the same; not in some tree-hugging hippie sense, but that the immigrant is the same as us precisely because we are all immigrants. And since all nations, and by extension peoples in a nation (especially those who believe in the notion of nationality, and national identity), have to find some manner, no matter what it is or from where it comes, to distinguish themselves from those around them, the other (in spite, and especially in the light, of its absence) is the most crucial aspect of the discourse of nationality. And in order to maintain the fantasy of *people from, of, the land* what also has to be maintained, through an act of exorcism, is the absolute otherness of the other.

There are very few moments when Boris Johnson is right. One of these rare instances can be found in his initial statement on Brevik: "it is not enough to say he is mad. Anders Breivik is patently mad."[15]

However, much like Breivik in his manifesto, he should have stopped whilst he was ahead. By attempting to diagnose Breivik —"the fundamental reasons for their callous behavior lie deep in their own sense of rejection and alienation. It is the ideology that gives them the ostensible cause … that gives them an excuse to dramatise the resentment … and to kill" — Johnson falls into the same trap that he accuses others of: "to try to advance any other explanation for their actions … is simply to play their self-important game." More importantly, and this is the point that Johnson completely misses, the attempt to rationalise Breivik's actions — to rehabilitate reason — is nothing other than a desperate attempt at maintaining his otherness.

In fact, we ended up going one step further: insisted on Breivik's sanity, put him on the stand, then accused him of displaying such a difference from all of us — through his indifference to human life — so we could rest safe that we were unlike him and his kind.

However, that is a dangerous game to play.

For, one should not forget that the turning point in Mary Shelley's *Frankenstein* is the moment when the monster speaks: at that very instance, the creature moves from an 'it' to a fully subjectivised person; with his own stories, historicities, emotions, and so on. And this is the moment where — echoing Žižek's reading of Shelley — "the ultimate criminal is thus allowed to present himself as the ultimate victim. The monstrous murderer reveals himself to be a deeply hurt and desperate individual, yearning for company and love."[16] But, in the case of Breivik, this goes beyond just a risk of us feeling for him: for, no one should deny another the opportunity to put forth her or his case. The problem lies with us trying to deny the madness of Breivik's act by putting him back under reason. The problem lies with our inability to differentiate the act from the person; the singular from the universal. And this is why Boris Johnson's plea was for us to ignore Breivik as a madman. But by doing so, Johnson conflates the notion of the act and the person; the singular and the universal — exactly the same gesture as insisting on his sanity: the 'madman' is merely the absolute other, one that we are not.

In our desperation to preserve the notion that we are rational beings incapable of becoming monsters, we had to deny the meaninglessness — in the strict sense of it lying outside of reason — of Breivik's act.

And in order to do so, we had to *provide meaning where there is none.*

For, if this act were a
moment of madness
— a moment that
comes from elsewhere

— we cannot say that it will not descend upon us one day. If Breivik's actions were that of a sane person, one who is in control of his being, his self, we can then locate the otherness in his being. More importantly, this would allow us to distinguish ourselves from that said being. Breivik's sanity is the only thing that allows us to say that 'this act of terror is born out of one with an ultra-right ideology'; and, perhaps more importantly, 'since I am not of that ideology, I would never do such a thing'. And by doing that, we attempt to protect ourselves by claiming that people who share Breivik's ideology are foreign to us, other to us.

However, if Breivik's act were a moment of insanity, his otherness is no longer locatable: and the notion of 'us and them' shifts from a geographical, physical, religious, or cultural notion, to one in the realm of ideas.

And this is what truly scares us.

For, if what is foreign is not phenomenological, then it cannot be seen, detected, sensed. Anders Behring Breivik terrifies us not merely for the fact that he was a white man in a white society, but more pertinently that his skin color did not matter: we would not have been able to spot him even if he were blue, even if he were right next to us, even if we had known him all our lives.

Even as we are grappling with holding Breivik accountable by declaring him of sound mind, what truly terrifies us is that deep down we know that Breivik's act is a moment of madness; beyond all comprehensibility. Which means that we would not be able to spot the idea; even if it were, at this very moment, in our heads.

Which might well be why there is still so much anger over Hannah Arendt's *Eichmann in Jerusalem*: not because she exonerated him (she did no such thing), but that she opened the dossier that it could have been any one of us. That all of us, any of us, could have been Adolf Eichmann.

Perhaps here, there is a lesson to be learned from Wes Craven's *A Nightmare on Elm Street*; where the most dangerous thing one could do, that could happen to one, was to mention, or hear of, Freddy's name. For, once you knew of him, you were open to the possibility of a visit, a visitation even, in your dreams. After which, it was a combination of external (if you die in your dreams, Freddy still lives; which suggests that he and you were separate) and internal (without you, there could be no Freddy; and the site of your death is your own dream) forces that determined your fate. However, regardless of whether one survived — even if one were victorious — it was one's knowledge that had brought about, is the necessary condition for opening, the possibility of one's death. Moreover, there is no actual way of definitively finishing-off Freddy: as long as someone, anyone, remembers him, as long as memory of him remained, there is always the possibility of his return, of him being recalled.

Thus, by concocting reasons, instead of compartmentalising, putting aside, one might well be doing nothing other than opening one's connection to whatever one was, is, attempting to reason away.

We have gone to great lengths to rehabilitate Breivik — and other such perpetrators of massive incomprehensible violence — in order to preserve our difference from them. What we really have been trying to deny is the fact that everyone, at any given moment, could have a moment of madness. And this is the true radicality of Mary Shelley: in allowing us to momentarily enter the head of the monster, she shows us not just the fact that he is like any one of us, but that any one of us could, in the right (or wrong) circumstance, be like him.

Which does not mean that one ignores everything —
not that one can, even if one attempts to do so.

But that, one keeps in mind that the problem
might well be the attempt to subsume everything
under reason in the first place. For, doing so
reduces, attempts to reduce, everything to *ratio*,
to measurement, calculation, calculability, an
accounting system; not that things — let alone events
— can be reduced, controlled. And here, it might
be apt to remind ourselves of Sylvère Lotringer's
reminder that *an event is like an earthquake*: it
comes when it comes, shakes us up, quite possibly
even ruptures us.[17] At best, one can attempt to
comprehend it after the fact; even then, it is but a
representation, nothing more. The event itself, like
"it is with the smallest earthquake, the least accident,
some terrorist act or other … are all equivalent in
the emergence of evil, in evil showing through like
an inalienable dimension, irreducible to the rational
order." [18]

Bang bang, he shot me down
Bang bang, I hit the ground
Bang bang, that awful sound
Bang bang, my baby shot me down.

— Sonny Bono[19]

This is the part that we all know and remember.

Whilst never quite remembering, this is a song that is not so much about violence, not really even about love, but about remembering.

For, after the bridge comes the accusatory stanza: "Now he's gone, I don't know why/ And till this day, sometimes I cry/ He didn't even say goodbye/ He didn't take the time to lie." *Bang Bang* is a game that the two lovers used to play; and all she has now is a memory of the game to remember him by. And the only reason she has to recall this game is: he never provided her a reason for leaving.

Not that she will, can, ever get a satisfactory answer.

And this is precisely the game we are playing with Anders Behring Breivik. For, even though he left a 1500 page manifesto, even though we allowed him to use the courtroom as his platform, we continued, will continue, screaming; will always continue to scream at him, *tell me why.*

For, what we want him to say — all we want him to tell us — is that we are not like him: all we really need him, are almost pleading with him, to do is, to "take the time to lie ..."

And, perhaps here, we should open our receptors to the echo of the *infans* resounding in *baby*. For, as Christopher Fynsk reminds us, the *infans* is one that is pre-language, pre-knowing, pre-understanding: it is the very finitude, and exteriority, of relationality itself.[20] And thus, it is a position of openness to the fullness of possibility — and nothing else.

For, the true horror of the 22nd of July, 2011, is the fact that it is not Anders Behring Breivik who is mad, but the act itself that is. And this is precisely why only "my baby" could have "shot me down." For, it is an act that is from beyond, a sheer act of madness that — as Plato warns us — is whispered into our ears (and can so easily be mistaken for inspiration, and even wisdom), an act that can both seize us, and cause us to cease, at the same time, in the very same moment.

And what can this utter openness to an other — the other — be, but a moment of love, a true *falling in love*.

Where, at the moment of the whisper, nothing can be known — for, we are babies as our baby shoots us down ….

For, one should never forget that, an event — "irreducible to the rational order" — is also no longer in the realm of morality.

An event is evil.

And it is a challenge.

To nothing other than morality,
to interpretation, understanding,
reason itself.

To answers.

Never forgetting that the first utterance of evil was quite possibly, "did God really say, you were not to eat of any of the trees in the garden'?"[21]

Perhaps, a "challenge."
Perhaps, more importantly — a question.

An unanswered question.

Quite possibly,
an unanswerable question.

To the apple itself.

Notes:

[1] 'Apple Announces iPhone 6 and iPhone 6 Plus
— the Biggest Advancements in iPhone History' &
'Apple unveils Apple Watch — Apple's Most Personal
Device Ever' in http://www.apple.com/hotnews/ (9
September, 2014)

[2] Juliet Eilperin & Ed O'Keefe. 'Obama announces
'broad coalition' to fight Islamic State extremist
group' in *The Washington Post* (10 September, 2014).

[3] BBC News. 'Ayman al-Zawahiri appointed as Al-
Qaeda leader.' (June 16, 2011).

[4] Yukari Iwatani Kane. 'Steve Jobs resigns as Apple
CEO' in *The Wall Street Journal* (August 25, 2011).

[5] Jean Baudrillard. *The Spirit of Terrorism*,
translated by Chris Turner. London: Verso, 2002: 10.

[6] George W. Bush. '9/11 address to the
nation' (September 11, 2011) in http://
www.americanrhetoric.com/speeches/
gwbush911addresstothenation.htm

[7] Slavoj Žižek. *Violence: Six Sideways Reflections*.
London: Profile Books, 2008: 150.

[8] Brad Stone & Josh Tyrangiel. 'Tim Cook Q&A:
The Full Interview on iPhone 6 and the Apple

Watch' in *Bloomberg Businessweek Technology* (19 September, 2014).

[9] *Ibid.*

[10] This statement was uttered by an unnamed Islamic State Jihadist during Medyan Dairieh's piece *The Islamic State* for VICE News, which can be found at https://news.vice.com/video/the-islamic-state-full-length

[11] This was captured during a rare public appearance by Abu Bakr al-Baghdadi in Medyan Dairieh's *The Islamic State.*

[12] Baudrillard. *The Spirit of Terrorism*, 12-13.

[13] Žižek. *Violence*, 34.

[14] *Ibid*: 35-36.

[15] Boris Johnson. 'Anders Breivik: There is nothing to study in the mind of Norway's mass killer' in *The Telegraph* (25 July, 2011).

[16] Žižek. *Violence*, 39.

[17] Lotringer reminded me of this during his seminar — entitled *Jean Baudrillard* — at the European Graduate School, August 2014.

[18] Jean Baudrillard. *The Intelligence of Evil or the Lucidity Pact*, translated by Chris Turner. Oxford: Berg Publishers, 2005: 186.

[19] Sonny Bono. 'Bang Bang (My Baby Shot Me Down)'. Los Angeles: Imperial Records, 1966.

[20] Christopher Fynsk. *Infant Figures: The Death of the Infans and Other Scenes of Origin*. Stanford: Stanford University Press, 2000.

[21] *Genesis* 3:1

Con tri but or s

Jeremy
Fernando

Jeremy Fernando is the Jean Baudrillard Fellow at the European Graduate School, where he is also a Reader in Contemporary Literature & Thought. He works in the intersections of literature, philosophy, and the media; and has written ten books — including *Reading Blindly*, *Living with Art*, and *Writing Death*. His work has also been featured in magazines and journals such as *Berfrois*, *CTheory*, *TimeOut*, and *VICE*, amongst others; and he has been translated into Spanish and Slovenian. Exploring other media has led him to film, music, and art; and his work has been exhibited in Seoul, Vienna, Hong Kong, and Singapore. He is the general editor of the thematic magazine *One Imperative*; and a Fellow of Tembusu College at the National University of Singapore.

Julian Gough

Julian Gough was born in London to Tipperary parents, and raised in Ireland. While studying philosophy at university in Galway, he began singing with the underground, and very literary, rock band Toasted Heretic. They played London, Paris and New York, released four albums, and had a top ten hit in Ireland in 1991 with 'Galway and Los Angeles', a song about not kissing Sinead O'Connor.

His first novel, *Juno & Juliet*, was published in the UK and US in 2001. His short story 'The Orphan and the Mob' won the BBC National Short Story Award (then the biggest prize in the world for a single story), in 2007.

His second novel, *Jude: Level 1*, was shortlisted for the 2008 Bollinger Everyman Wodehouse Award, alongside work by Alan Bennett, Garrison Keillor and Will Self. (The *Sunday Tribune* described it as "possibly the finest comic novel since Flann O'Brien's *The Third Policeman*.")

His story 'The Great Hargeisa Goat Bubble' was the first short story ever published by the *Financial Times*. It was subsequently adapted into a radio play by the BBC.

In early 2010, the *Sunday Tribune* chose *Jude: Level 1* as their Irish Novel of the Decade.
His collected poems and lyrics, *Free Sex Chocolate*, were published by Salmon in 2010.
He represented Ireland in the Dalkey Archive anthology, *Best European Fiction 2010*, and in 2011, he wrote the ending to Time Magazine's computer game of the year, *Minecraft*, broadcast his second radio play, 'The Great Squanderland Roof', on BBC Radio 4, and published his third novel, *Jude in London*, which was again shortlisted for the Bollinger Everyman Wodehouse Award.

In 2013, he had a UK Number One Kindle Single with his novella, *CRASH! How I Lost A Hundred Billion And Found True Love.*

Julian now lives in Berlin.

He is probably best known for stealing Will Self's pig.

Neil Murphy

Neil Murphy teaches contemporary literature at NTU, Singapore. He is the author of *Irish Fiction and Postmodern Doubt* (2004) and editor of *Aidan Higgins: The Fragility of Form* (2009). He co-edited (with Keith Hopper) the special Flann O'Brien centenary issue of the *Review of Contemporary Fiction* (2011) and *The Short Fiction of Flann O'Brien* (2013). He has also published articles and book chapters on contemporary fiction, Irish writing, and theories of reading. His co-edited *Dermot Healy's Collected Fiction*, and *Dermot Healy: Writing the Sky — Critical Essays and Observations* will both be published by Dalkey Archive Press in 2015.

Tan
Jingliang

Tan Jingliang (b. 1990, Malaysia) completed her BFA in film at Nanyang Technological University in 2013; where she had been awarded the Nanyang Scholarship. Her graduate short film *The Transplants* premiered at the 43rd International Film Festival Rotterdam. In 2014, she attended the Asian Film Academy in Busan, South Korea, where she was mentored by the Hungarian auteur Béla Tarr; and was also awarded the New York Film Academy Scholarship in Beijing. She lives and works in Singapore.

Yanyun Chen

Yanyun Chen is a Ph.D. candidate at the European Graduate School. She received the Lee Kuan Yew Gold Medal Award and the Nanyang Scholarship for her undergraduate degree in animation from the Nanyang Technological University, Singapore. She has been trained at the Florence Academy of Art in Sweden, The Animation Workshop in Denmark, and under Miroslav Trejtnar and Zdar Sorm in the Czech Republic. She was an *artist-in-residence* at Hackerspace Singapore, and Tembusu College, at the National University of Singapore; where she developed animated short films and games. The eco-awareness game *Jimmyfish,* created with a team of friends, exhibited at the Japan Media Arts Festival 2012 and was awarded the Jury Selection Award.

Her current research revolves around drawing, etymology, and continental philosophy.

Her practice is rooted in the craft of making things.

CPSIA information can be obtained at www.ICGtesting.com
Printed in the USA
BVIW12n0056180515
400604BV00004B/12